Loveruage

a dance in three parts

Loveruage

a dance in three parts

Ashok Mathur

Wolsak and Wynn

Copyright © Ashok Mathur, 1994
All rights reserved. No part of this book may be
reproduced or transmitted in any form, by any means,
electronic or mechanical, without permission in writing
from the publisher, except by a reviewer who may quote
brief passages in a review.

Part one of *Loveruage* was published by West Coast Line
in 1992.

Typeset in Bookman, printed in Canada by The Coach
House Press, Toronto. Author's photo by Ashok Mathur.
Cover art by Shani Mootoo

The publishers gratefully acknowledge support by
The Canada Council, Multiculturalism and Citizenship
Canada, and The Ontario Arts Council.

Wolsak and Wynn Publishers Ltd., Post Office Box 316
Don Mills, Ontario, Canada, M3C 2S7

Canadian Cataloguing in Publication Data
Ashok Mathur, 1961-
  Loveruage, a dance in three parts
Poems.
ISBN 0-919897-38-X
I. Title.
PS8576.A86L68 1994   C811'.54   C94-931254-1
PR9199.3.M37L68 1994

from and for Sonia

one

into
skin

Ho and the story begin to here. No story to beginning there before. But cause this is the way it happened, and I can't make it up if I try. It was happening this sort long ago but cause ten years back least that and when I would have kill my own self if wasn't for the sing. Ready to go as was but cause for the sing and the sleep and the branch but but but cause. Happened so fast so ago so I'm here try to telling this story but the words caughting but cause up up in the high highing branches which did saving my life. And so that look. Yes yeahyes I've been see that looking before always always when I begin of talking but cause no one can see be seeing what I say oh say now. When I first begin to speaking so in this way this new way in this new place from far far from where I being child, I yes but cause be get looking from all you all you just as now. But cause but you sit and wait for me I be changing changing all the time and soon you hearing the language you wait but cause for so long oh yeah. When I look forward seeing, look forward my talk and talking all of this but cause, but, so I have to be shift-like and look back when it was now and all different and not so hard as then. When it was now, ten years after.

When it was now, after years of learning and speaking and writing.

When it was now, a full decade after.

When it was now, and here I am, ten years older and growing older still, thanks to what happened those long years ago. And words are so different for me now.

> *Standing. Stilling. Swaying. Breezing. Standstillswaybreeze. Leaves falling. Sap slowing. Air cooling. Leavesfall sapslow aircool. Rope burn cut slice. Standing. Still.*

Back then, when I was new here, everything seemed new here. So much action and speed. What a picture I was, dowdy and dazed, standing on the bus platform like I'd just stepped out of a Unesco postcard. My cousin said she'd be there but she wasn't. This was the new world. My new world. Everything full of action and speed and I was dazzled by the whiteness of it all.

"Say man, you lost?"
"?"
"I mean, ma'am —?"
"Gnugh!?"
"Cuz if you're lost or somethin'..."

"*Ujana sudhana.*" River flowing river river current up against, this is what I mean, this is my voice, choose the path of resistance, up against the current, swimming hard, banging off the waves, bouncing off the rocks, and make the path my own.

"I'm sorry? Well, take it easy ma'am — or, I mean..."

The young man was only trying to be helpful. He was my introduction to a spotless, unscented world. It wasn't his fault that he didn't know whether I was man or woman. At home I was — but no, that was there, the past, the dead past, and this was the here and now and I was whatever this new world gave me. I was greeted on the platform with a man-ma'am and I took the first step, first stroke, *ujana sudhana*, against the current. At home I was — but here I was newnamed and I became Manam. My cousin never did come that day and I left the platform by myself.

You left the platform by yourself. And you were by yourself for so many years. You were oogyana sa-dana? is that right? fighting against the current, going against the flow. To have known you then, to have met you then. When you were coming off that platform. Before everything happened. It must have been awful. Feel for you, really do. You were so fresh, as you say, a photograph come to life from a third-world postcard.

You must have been so beautiful. Must have been, huh. You are, you are beautiful, see it in you, emanating from you. Knew it when first saw you. Standing there, you were alone again, and your eyes were full of sorrow and love and couldn't help but fall in love. Watching you standing there; said:

"Couldn't help noticing you, sorrysorry, don't mean to be rude, but areyou areyou waiting for somebody?"

And you said: "Uh-uh. Jus' standin' here." Just like that, you said that jus' standin' here, and couldn't help (couldanyone?) couldn't help but fall in love with that sorrow in your eyes. Had to be with you. Had to love you. You, such a beautiful ... beautiful ... beautiful Manam....

I floated for a long time. Uglily. A spotted and darkened blot on a frothy white sea, pristine white sea, clean oh so clean that's what it was, the world I was in. And I was an aberration, an abomination on this frothy surface. And I floated uglily for a long time.

"Do you have any skills?"

"Scellz?"

"Skills. Abilities. What can you do?"

"Do? Do. I can doing anything all sorts. Work in all sorts all sorts, all have. All can doing but cause if any help help..."

"All sorts? Like a handy— person? Well, that would come in ... handy. Sure. Uh, do you have any education?"

"?"

"EDuCAtion? Training. School?"

"Ah school, but cause no good teacher if to teach the small childs with speak speaking this very very hard."

"No, have you *had* any training, formal training as a handy, or whatever, anything. Ms ... ter? I'm sorry, it doesn't say here whether you're, well..."

"Manam."

"Yes, well, M–anam, then. It's very difficult for us to place someone without knowing exactly what they can do."

"Work hard but cause need knowing how to speak then all will be righting all will be."

"Yes. It will be."

"Yes."

But no. It was hardly an easy road. I floated in and out of the froth, working where I could and playing the roles asked of me. I had come from a world where nothing was asked and I had chosen to come here. And here they asked me to cleanse myself, to cleanse myself and purify the world I had come into. They asked this of me.

They asked this of you. You have told of this. How you floated between jobs as a manthenawoman but always as Manam. They asked you to clean yourself, you said, clean yourself and the world you were in. You tell, laughing now, how you began cleaning toilets at the bus station, the same station you first came to. And you went from there to cleaning floors. Then you cleaned windows. Then you moved to an office building, and late at night, when all the office workers were safely sleeping, you told how you'd clean from floor to floor. And that's where you were written, wasn't it? That's where you said it happened and kept on happening and hearing that, you telling that, there were tears here so many tears. Nothing to do.

> *Whisperly rustle. Tenderly twirling. Autumnly waiting. Desperately dormant. Whisperhiss. Tendertensed. Autumnugly. Desperatedying.*
> *Whispertenderautumndesperate. Ropely sweet sensation undercutly into bark.*

I would work there in the office tower, darkened but for the perpetual light from the tubing in the hall. Work hard. And in the days I'd read the books I'd find, a glutton for the words that would one day wash away the smell of vinegar and lye. And yes I learned. Learned to speak the way the new world wanted me to speak. Learned to forget that *ujana sudhana* was my mentor, and that my true learning came as I soaped and scrubbed the floors walls desks doors. And when I met Him who would teach me more than I ever wished to know.... He was tall and large and His eyes were a smoggy grey and when I looked at them I was looking through Him. My shift was nearly over that morning. I was on my last floor, emptying waste paper baskets and, as I always did, seizing wads of computer sheets to practice my writing. I had a box of paper in my hands when I felt His presence.

"Wht th hll r y'dng?"

"Nothing, sir no sir nothing but cause going throw 'way and all so put for using in."

"Tht's cmpny prprty, ya stpd ful."

"Sir, yesyes sorry nothing but cause..."

"Gdm thf, shd kc sm sns'n tayou."

I couldn't protect myself against the butterfly quickness and unpredictability of His words. They flew at me, landed angrily, then before I could grasp them they were replaced by new, yet more unfamiliar sounds.

"Foreigner, gv nch tk mile, tch a lsn, tch ya gd." His face was pink and hot and so close I could feel the sweat leach from his pores; and my face, brown and smooth, passively bore his exhaustive torrent of verbal violence. Acquiescing, I bowed my head, to show respect, to acknowledge defeat and wrongness. And that's when words grew louder and blastier and when they stopped the silence was worse, for there He stood, breathing hate and closeness into my flesh my mind my

He was there forever and when He left I eased my body to the floor. He was gone. I could still hear and fear his words in my head. Banging and insistent. Compared to those words inside my body, his silence was nothing. But it stayed with me, shrouded around me. I rose. There were bootmarks, his, on the computer paper. I took that with me and, later that afternoon, over the stained, warped surface, copied neat lines of verse from a damaged and discarded book of modernist verse I had found in the garbage of a second-hand bookstore. My letters were neat and perfectly formed that afternoon.

Your letters were perfectly formed that day. And you continued to copy lines of poetry and prose from thrown-out books you had found. And you got better at writing on thrown-out computer paper from the office tower where you still worked. And every night, or almost every night, he was there and he would attack you with his words and then his breath and awful silence, and then his mouth would ooze more spit and filth upon you. But you kept going to work. You kept going and he kept coming. You said he was enjoying it now, unleashing those words on you like he could do to no one else. You said the standing silent, the breathy quiet, was not so bad, would not have been so bad, if it hadn't been preceded, always, by those words. Words tongued into your skin, welted into your body. But you kept going back. Going back. Why did you keep going back?

> *Braided branded sucked stucked rope into limb into side into skin. Wrapped warped corpsed cutted. Into*

I. I remember. I remember that night. I remember that night He came and He cut and He wrote.

"Thr y r s-hole, cm her so'i cn shw y smthng spshl."

"But cause this is nevernever bad thing, I working so good and cannot bear very much reality but cause."

He turned out the light so the office was dark and all I could see was the pinky glow from His face and a grey light from His eyes. In His hand was a letter opener with a grey blade and I knew this time there would be no standing there silence, no quiet after the words.

"Dm bch. Bch? r y mn or wmn? Hrd t tl wth those clothes on." And in the pinkgrey light from His face the blade came toward me and His hand reached out ripping tearing and the knife ripping tearing dully pulling shredding and and and He stood above me laughing spitting words and letters incomprehensible unconnected and then the letter opener coming closer to my body naked body open body blank unwritten body. And in

the dark, lit only by the pinkgrey of his face,
he began to write upon my skin with that dull
blade words full words no mistaking them
now, words I remembered painfully writing
myself on bootstamped sheets of stolen
computer paper and I could hear these words
well, I could read these words in my body
well, the vowels and consonants and carefully
scribed syllables, written into me, and me,
stonestill, fascinated, the bloodly ink
obscuring obfuscating then revealing letters in
my skin. He wrote my death into my body.

    He wrote your death into your body. But
he did not write you into death. He did not
write you to death. He left you alone,
ashamed, writhing with the writing on your
bloody skin. The morning light was pinkgrey,
too, but brighter than his face, and horrified
workers saw you written on the office floor.

You stood and clothed yourself, covered the words, and forever left the building of your learning. You walked to your home and you filled a bag with doubly inscribed computer paper. You took a rope. You walked far far and through the day and no words came to you except what words were with you and then it was evening and the city was behind. You saw the grove and you saw the tree. You touched its bark its coarsely written skin. You began to climb.

> *Stroke and stride. Cleave and climb.*
> *Breathe and brush. Rush and rope.*
> *strokecleavebreatherush*
> *strideclimbbrushrope*

    I ascended with the rope. I touched the hoary bark and clawed words into the cracks; written bark clawed back and overwrote upon my skin. I reached the topmost branch and sat with words in me and over me. I tied the rope around the limb, tied it tight, and let the rope hang loose below. In setting sun the rope was silhouetted, a hanging silent O. I touched the coarseness of the rope the roughness of the bark the toughness of my skin and lay my head to rest upon the tree.

> *Sleepdreamriserest wordless wondrous dream a dream of life dream a dream of wordless wondrousity dream a dream of dreams dream into a life dream away from death undeathed dream*

You lay your head to rest upon the tree and when you woke the sky was dark and words had come and gone and would not hurt you now. You say the tree began to sing, a wordless song, singing to you in your sleep, song and sing and soft inside your ear. You came down from the tree and looked up at the O and smiled your gratitude. You burned the words you had so carefully inscribed on computer paper and left the ashes as an offering for your life. And two days later you were standing there, saw you standing there and you were beautiful, full of sorrow, but beautiful, too beautiful for words and who could not love you?

The words inside my skin are softer now. They fade and fall away with every passing day. We go back to the tree now.
I see her in the grove and know that she is taller now. Up up so high silhouetted by the sky I see the O, still there, speaking to me wordlessly. O. O. O. I touch her written skin and sing the song she sang to me and then begin to climb her slowly stilly.

I have no words I have no sex I have no song
but what she sang to me singing softly
Manam Manam Manam

> *Manam ma'am, no man wo man curl
> unfurl me let me breathe untie me sift
> me sing me touch and tinge me manam
> manam manam*

Singing softly Manam manam manam,
you fall asleep upon the branch, the singing
limb, and breathe and listen wordlessly and
under watchful eye you wake and wonder
touch the aged O.

The rope is old and weathered but hangs
there still. The limb is written into by the
loop, the rope writes words upon the branch
and I say O. I try untie the rope but fast it
holds, imprinted on the tree I work unwork

pull push try hard but cause no way grows there inside no way is buried so so but cause not worked and words worded in the tree unsinged pull but never never but cause and I say yes this happening just so but cause you never gonna believe this when I tell you, but I can't never make it up if I try. Never.

two

into
loveruage

Yes, there you were, standing there in pose as if you had always been standing there, statuesque sorrow, waiting for my arrival. And so damn beautiful. So beautiful no words could ever touch the truth you told to me, that day, standing there alone and sorrowed. Yes, there you were. And I came to you unspeakingly and touched your shoulder, cold, and pulled your eyes. And so we met.

That day, that was such a day, we met and never said a word. I did not know what I mistook for thoughtful air, a wordlessness that came from you, was not a fact of silence but of volumes written out to you, on you, in you. And we walked in this wordfilled silence down a thousand misty bridges into morning fog and we had steps of children and of each other. We walked to each other's stride, carefully, and always so unspokenly. I began to fabricate a story, my story, which after hours became the true story, of how your vocal chords were lost so long ago and words meant nothing to you now, words were only spaces to fill the power of your silence, and you would not bow to that. My story had you vowing yourself into quiet, leaving the hard-edged, crisp-toned world that I had known as home, and taking yourself away to a world that knew no sound, no language, no voice.

And I knew I was right. And you let me believe so. And then you let drop the sorrow from your eyes, and in a moment of unbelievable light, lips still unparted, you took me into your sound.

"Blood."
"WHAT?"
"( )"
"You spoke. You spoke. You said. You said blood?"
"( )"
"You did. I thought you couldn't speak. But you said blood, I know you did, I heard you say it, Ohmygod, you spoke. Say it again, please? What did you mean, 'Blood'? That's what you said, isn't it? It is, tell me it is."

But your face was back into itself again, and there we were, standing there, facing each other, me snapping word after word at you, and you with your eyes hidden by the shadow of your brow, stone-still and saying nothing. We were like that for ages, hours, yes, I'm sure. Me fumbling for words that were covered over by silence, and you, one word escaping, living with the words covered by your shawl.

I watched you. And I loved you. Then, if not before, before we began our walking over bridges and into misty mornings. For certain then. And so your hand came out from under that earthgrey shawl and seemed to move without your body to brush back the shadows from your eyes. And I saw. And your hand moved across the surface of your body, down past chest and belly and hip, and with a gesture that was not there, touched without touching between your legs.

"Blood."
"Blood?"
"Blood."

I did not wonder, then, as perhaps I should have, whether the blood you spoke was the flow of your body or the unnatural loss from a wound. You spoke without sorrow or joy. You spoke your blood as the body speaks. And your blood and your voice touched my ear and mind with a softness which made me not question who you were or from where came your blood. I only listened to your blood and heard your hand sweep down and in touching yourself engulf my body too.

And as if we knew each other's bodies, if not words, we turned to search out more bridges.

This was a dream to me, my love, your body come into mine as a dream. Your blood flowed inside me and warmed me and pulsed me. And when the time came, when you stopped, stared, and began laughing deeply,

I laughed too, and I did not know why, but I knew I was right to laugh. So, together, our throats gurgled and our diaphrams heaved and we sank to the wet pavement uncaring for our clothes or our bodies, laughing. Your hand rose again, again not part of your body, but always part of you, and you pointed to the building we sat beside. The mist was heavy now and I could see only a grey outline in a grey evening. The building was square, consistent, a block of grey ever so slightly darker than the surrounding mist. A huge browngrey centre marked its doorway, oaken and shut. And your finger pointed.

"This is the sky."
"The sky?"
"The sky. This is."
"This church. Is the sky. ?"
"This, the sky."

And your arm, still outstretched, finger pointing as if in accusation, went taut and frozen, and I read the sky in your hand. Did we rise and walk, or did the mist carry us? We were inside, and your arm was still raised in salute to the sky, and all around us were oak pews.

"Pebbles to the sea."

I would have sworn the pews themselves trembled to your words. We were the only sound in the church which I knew for certain was the sky. And the pews were now pebbles to the sea. There was no other choice. Pebbles to the sea in the sky and your words were never clearer. Floated: you did, you floated down the aisle to the altar, although I knew better than to call this an altar. I waited for your words. You surveyed the scene, eyes passing over a stained pulpit to the crucified sculpture hanging above. I knew your words were a judgement and a naming and I knew I would never not understand again. Your shawl slipped off your shoulders and a cruel pink glow blew from your back, words stunning me with their force, glancing off me with their brilliance, sinking into me with their sound. You wore a thousand words inside your skin, and I knew they were not your words but would always have to be your words. You had been named and unnamed so many times a palimpsest was where your skin should be. And so, the words already screaming from your body, you began to speak to, to name, the figure on the cross.

"Voice.
Voice. Leaves. Cacophony. Sticky
   silence.
voice
leaves
cacaphony
sticky silence
hoarfrost
ujana sadhana
blade of grass
odes to a canteloupe
variations on an I
holes become emblems of personal
  property
go ye forth and procreate and sin
  abundantly
sa!
but cause
dancer kills the dance in holy
  matrimony

seek and ye shall falter
smell these words in blood"

And on you spoke, words frothing from your throat, describing, explaining, articulating the love and death inside your words inside your body. You spoke and spat a hatred of language by abusing the language, yet you could not, would not, forgive yourself the penalty of silence as you wreathed the carved statue who remained silent throughout. Before pebbles to the sea. In the sky. And when you finally turned to me, the words turned with you and you bled into my eyes and once again I swam in love for you. You crossed pebbles and walked through sky and ignored the crashing sea to reach me and your holes became my holes, emblems of personal property, us to each other. You killed me with a dance of words and what we

sought was seen by many as a sin to our flesh
(the flesh of the same should never be brought
together). You sang me words of absurdity,
let them drop into silence, our bodies through
our eyes and mouths were sticky and I did not
know where I had become you, and all of the
mist outside sank into my thigh and all
around were leaves and hoarfrost and a blade
of grass invaded my sight and entered my
body.

    Swirling. We sinned.

    First with words. Then with bodies.

    Then with both.

    I read your back with my tongue. Words
interrupted each other, silenced and cancelled
each other, interrogated my lips and fingers
and melted into my throat.

    No words of ecstasy were allowed out.
They were uttered but they stayed within the
sky. They were spoken but only as pebbles to

the sea. They were voiced but became a pattern on your back for your reclamation. And mine.

I lay upon your words, breathing thoughts to myself.

"I."

I listened to you speak my name.

"I."

You spoke without speaking and the letter of my self was scrawled high into my thigh, grazing me closely with a soft razor shadow.

"I. A yearning. I."

I breathed back yearning but would not speak. Dare not.

Body's blood throbbed through us. You spoke of yearning in a church that was the sky, amongst oak pews (where believers could never sit again) which were pebbles to the sea, beneath a hanging figure who had witnessed the more gracious acts of shared words and bodies than had ever before been witnessed. You breathed words onto my back and I breathed the words upon your back. We slid our bodies into language and we languaged our bodies to each other. And again, in that holy space that was the sky, we found pebbles in each other and took them to the sea.

three

———

into
our

———

We

bhum

us

bhumm

our

bhummm

standing still together in a high darkness
surrounded by a thousand drums all who
bhum for

an ending of sorts to recount a beginning

---

an ending of sorts to discount a beginning

an ending of sorts to count on beginning

again.

Ho and the story to end here. No story to ending before there. Sometimes go backback is to forward trace. No no no no story in here unless a beginning cause the end and no no no story in here unless the end start the beginning. And when it go back way back to the end of time after the story begun, way back before the acorn and before the humus and before the rock break down into growearth, way back before before before the

there was the

you hear the

and sound the

bhum
bhum
bhum

stretch and draw and tighten taut
pull you close over my body my vessel my self
draw tight tauten seal down and tie
hemp yourself onto around into over

and
bhum

bhum

,went your voice and you sang into me with deepness and sadness and breathness and song.

bhum.

This is the memory: a blackness in front of us all, a raised blackness smelling of earth and wet and the smell of the not-yet-born and the heartbeat murmurs of passion and sleep. This is the memory: white light drifting down in sashes to the raised earth, white light flaking over the blackness with erratic precision, white light centering a path for you to follow up from your cloud under the earth. This is the memory: you fade in with the light, on the light, slender your body up into the earth, and the white light touches your skin with smoke and salt falls from our eyes without water as we watch.

This is the memory: your hands around wood
so old and weary it grafts itself to your palms.
This is the memory: a drift of palm and skin
and wood toward the black dark now light, to
the contour of your face.
This is the memory: from the dark rises
tightened skin, stretched taut, smooth wood.
This is the memory: from the light falls
oldened wood grafted to tight skin.
This is the memory: wood and skin meets
skin and wood.
This is the memory: skin and wood meets
wood and skin.
This is the memory: wood and skin and wood
and skin. Meet.

bhum.
bhum.

bhum.
bhum BHUM bhum BHUM bhum BHUM
BHUM BHUM.

*stretch me taut and woodtouch and skintaut
and touch of wood on skin of wood of skin
surrounding murmur filled and hollow bringing
down a sound of*

bhum

And the story now humming in my ears, it's
nearly done and not nearly begun the sound
of my skin on my wood in my ear. With my
hand a piece of wood and the sky the colour
of dark and the skin on my face and the skin
on the wood all the same, and most of all, you
before the dark, hearing you wet to my skin
and my hand brought the wood to the skin.
The sound I uttered was not from my throat

but it was, and it was not from my hand or
my skin or the sky, no it was. The sound kept
me hungry and nourished and thirsty for the
wet skin of yours in my mouth. And the
wood. Oh, the wood. I wrapped around the
wood and felt the grain with my tongue and
the tightness of your flesh was the head of the
drum

bhum
bhum
bhum
bhum BHUM bhum BHUM BHUM BHUM
bhum bhum bhum
bhum
bhum

This is the memory: you coming into the
mists from the dark and the light and your
skin on the wood on the skin on the wood

touch me play   touch   play me
  touch me play   o

O, when it was now, after years of learning and speaking and writing.

 O, when it was now, ten years after.

 O, when it was now, and here I am, older and growing older still, because of the years gone by and their favour. And things are so strangely the same for me now.

Was it really so short ago I left myself standing on the platform where no train, no cousin, would ever arrive. Was it really so short ago I said to that voice, "uh-uh, jus' standin' here," and that voice took me into itself and loved me for, as said, for being beautiful without measure? Was it really so

short ago a blind of office towers and
wastepaper and consonantal incisions
sheared into my skin as I waited to language
the body of myself into a world who was my
new sea? Was it really so short ago a silence
in the sky became pebbles to the sea and the
word of blood emerged from my mouth and
resonated in my body from my centre from my
skin? And was it really so short ago my
tongue found language in the skin of a

bhum

bhum

bhum

You left the church with a passion glowing in
your face like the blood of fire. (What has
happened to my language? I speak what I

used to feel but all my voice comes out as if it were you?) No, there was no church. We left the sky and were as pebbles to the sea.

But there is more, much more. We retreated. You retreated. To that place you called the place of your rebirth. To the place you called that place of your blood. To a place where

sing to me child sing to my skin on my skin to me child
sink to my skin and do sing to me sink to me sing
child
sing the song of my skin

To a place where I was born, where my blood came to the surface of my skin and flowed through my song. I took you with me there to the sacred o again to the singing of the skin

---

and the singing of the blood from my back
and my throat. And this is where it began all
over and this is how it began, though you
never gonna believe this when I tell you, but I
can never make it up if I try. Never. She sang
me into her death, and that's the truth for
certain, even though who sings her own
death? She begged me climb again, to find
my place in her skin, to sing my blood over
her limbs so fine so fine. And so again this
happened, not like before, exactly like before, I
begin to find her shape with my hands, my
feet, my tongue, my lips, my body whole body,
touching her on the skin whose skin was
rougher and gentler than mine.

*sing to me child sing to my skin on my skin to
me child*
sink to my skin and

bhum
bhum

And I sang in her skin and I wore her skin on my tongue, yes I did. And I rose in her song, and I rose, as I rose, you too sang before her and me at the base. You sang with your smoke and your fire and skin all your own. You took on another's fine body and mind as you sang with your skin, wrapped tight round your wood, and your song was so soft and so sounding and wounding your song was a selfless sound

bhum
bhum

bhum bhum bhum bhum

Your body was smoke as it rose in her, rose in her, and I was the fire beneath. My last mind and body were lost in the wind, and I watched and I played and I sang your retreat.
Watched you rise in the skin and the blood of your rain. I would swear then, but that was then, that I heard the song too. But now I remember I sang my own skin on its wood and with smoke and with fire, that's all I could hear. But her song was there too I am sure.

sing to me child sing my skin over skin and
sing in me sink in me sing
sing to my sky and to blood and to leaves and
to breath in me
sing child
now sing child
now sing

bhum bhum

And my blood carried me up in her high to the cradle. This was the cacophony, this was the hoarfrost, this was the smell of these words in the blood. *Ujana sadhana.* Then sleep came. She gave to me sleep. And dreams. Dreams of voices in the blood of the silence. The loveruage in her language, the o in her skin, and the waking was a birth of me again.

sing me forever child
sing my skin forever
sink into me and sing into me for
ever
child
sing, sink, child
sing, sink
SA!

You woke with a start, resting in the limbs
which once so long ago held the aged O. You
woke with a start in your eye, and your mouth
formed an O and uttered it silently. You
pulled from the skin and with blood in your
face and the words on your back your body
rose up from its place. Tall and high you
were, and I was at the base of the tree in the
smoke and the smell of your skin. And you
said

SA! A word that came from nowhere. This
was a word without meaning, a word without
conscience. The sound was a word not
inscribed on my back, but a word from the
tree. She had given me life and now she gave
me a word that was death and completion and
song. The tree was my lifesource and
deathsource and dance. And of course, she
was always my song.

*sing me down now child   sink words into my
skin child
sing me to my O child   sing me down now
sing me down now
sing me
down*

bhum bhum bhum

And standing there, at the base of the tree, at the base of the O and the base of your skin, my mouth was awide with your birth and her death. My blood poured from pores and from glands and from ducts. The sky opened me up and slid pebbles to the sea.

SA! I said aloud to you and to her. And the silent syllable cut through the O, cut through the skin, cut through the blood and the sky to the sound of the skin on my back. *SA!!*

Cutting through and into wood. Skin opened
up and the words unworded skin. In the
smoke and the fire the word had the power.
SA!! sa. Carving calmly a song from the side
of her skin. A deft remarker. And an imprint
of song from the words unhealed on my back.

bhum
bhum
bhum bhum bhum bhum bhum

sing me into song   child
sing me into skin

In the smoke and the black now you rise with
the wood and the skin. No words in you now,
just the light and the sound of the drum. No
words in your back, just the words in the skin
of her skin of your skin of your

bhum
bhum
bhum

Ho and the story to end here. No story to ending before there. Sometimes go backback is to forward trace. No no no no story in here unless a beginning cause the end and no no no story in here unless the end start the beginning. And when it go back way back to the end of time after the story begun, way back before the acorn and before the humus and before the rock break down into growearth, way back before before before the skin get get get skin get get get get into skin

bhum
bhum
bhum
bhum